The EUREKONOMICS™
Dazzling Dozen

The overlooked and under-reported benefits

of participating whole life insurance.

by Jeffrey Reeves, MA

The EUREKONOMICS™
Dazzling Dozen
by Jeffrey Reeves, MA

For more information, contact Poor Richard Publishing
1270 Jasmine St., Denver CO 80220 — (303)355-0550
Jeffrey.Reeves@USA.net
Published by Poor Richard Publishing Co. Denver, CO
Printed in the United States of America
1st Printing

Author: Jeffrey Reeves, MA
Graphic Design: Sandra Reeves of Poor Richard Publishing Co.

13-digit ISBN: 978-0-9797709-4-4
10-digit ISBN:0-9797709-4-7
Library of Congress Control Number : 2011921370

iii

Table of Contents

Introduction

For the past three decades or so the number of companies offering participating whole life insurance contracts has declined. The decline did not occur because participating whole life insurance was a bad product or because the companies that sell participating whole life insurance are bad companies.

Quite the opposite is true. The most respected companies in the insurance business — even today — are the mutual companies that sell highly effective participating whole life insurance policies:

- » Lafayette Life
- » Northwestern Mutual
- » Massachusetts Mutual
- » Mutual Trust Life
- » New York Life
- » Ohio National Life
- » One America
- » The Guardian Life Insurance Company,
- » other companies that offer participating policies.

The decline was not the result of the failure of these companies to promote these products to their representatives; nor did it result from the failure of other mutual companies (Metropolitan, Prudential, John Hancock, and The Principal Financial Group as examples) to survive the onslaught of the EF Hutton universal life attack on the insurance industry and the A.L. Williams rape of mutual whole life insurance policies to extract their cash values to fund failed strategies. The E.F. Hutton and A.L. Williams misadventures, however, contributed to the problem and led to the complete destruction of companies like Mutual Benefit Life, one of the oldest and most respected among the old line mutuals, and others that failed or fell to acquisition.

No. The decline came because the mutual life insurance industry succumbed to the thinking of Wall Street in lieu of the reality of main street; it failed to protect its deserved and revered position as the source of advice and products that Americans could rely on as a foundation for their financial security, the bed rock of their peace of mind, and the framework for their futures.

It's time to reinstate what remains of the mutual life insurance industry — and perhaps motivate the formation of new mutual insurance businesses — as the leading voices for America's personal economies. It's time to resurrect the use of participating whole life insurance as the essential element in every American's financial structure. It's time to drag American's — kicking and screaming if necessary — out of the uncharted financial swamp created by the failures of the universal life experiments of the 80's and 90's and back onto the solid ground that only participating whole life insurance provides.

This essay addresses twelve compelling reasons why you should place participating whole life insurance at the foundation of your financial house or, if you are an advisor, why you should present this class of product to your clients. This essay outlines the principles and practices such policies support and the benefits of following those practices. We call this EUREKONOMICS™. Do not let the conventional wisdom that participating whole life insurance is a bad place to put money blind you from seeing and understanding the truth.

There is no other financial product that is as powerful, versatile and flexible as participating whole life insurance. Denying this product and its capabilities to yourself — or to your clients if you are an advisor — is not in anyone's best interests.

Jeffrey Reeves — January 2011, Denver, Colorado

The Dazzling Dozen – No. 1

Reason number one why you and every money-smart person should choose to build your personal economy with participating whole life insurance at its core:

The cash value build-up in participating whole life insurance policies lets you be your own *bank*.[1] You can get to the money from your whole life policy whenever you want it or need it…no penalties, no waiting, no taxes.

Most financial products are designed by Behemoths that want to build their own portfolio of "money under management." Their reasons are easy to understand. The Behemoths want to hoard as much money as possible in their own coffers. That way they can earn commissions on transactions, charge fees and hang onto profits in excess of the expected returns. Because of this, many of the products they sell tend to place significant restraints on your ability to access your own money without incurring penalties or waiting for some arbitrary date to arrive.

In addition, some financial products either are or can be incorporated into "qualified" plans. That usually means you can take a tax deduction when you put money into the plan.

---

1   The word *bank* is intended only to describe the processes of EURKONOMICS™ and does not imply that someone following these principles and practices is a chartered commercial bank.

1

It also means that you can't get your money out of the plan without paying penalties and taxes.

Everyone experiences events in life that demand immediate access to money. For many, the money they have in qualified plans is the only money available when one of life's surprisingly unsurprising surprises comes along. The result: penalties, taxes and starting all over again.

There is a better way.

Money you hold in a participating whole life insurance contract — your EUREKONOMICS™ *bank* — is easily accessible. It usually takes only a phone call to the insurance company to get a check written and in the mail; no penalties, no waiting, no taxes. There are not normally any fees associated with the transaction. And, you can usually replace the money you take out without penalty and without compromising the integrity of your policy.

Here's an example from my own experience. My daughter turned 16 — guess where this is going — and got her driver's license. A few months later she was allowed to drive my brand new Oldsmobile to school for the first time. A ditch, two fences and a concrete bird-bath later, I was staring at over $7,000.00 damage, a $1,000.00 deductible and a $1230.00 per year insurance premium increase. Thank goodness I had participating whole life insurance. I borrowed the money quickly to pay the deductible and increased car insurance premium.

The Dazzling Dozen – No. 2

Reason number two why you and every money-smart person should choose to build your personal economy with participating whole life insurance at its core:

The government, your employer, or any other outsiders have nothing to say about how you operate your EUREKONOMICS™ program.

When you put your money in a commercial bank it is subject to the whims of your bank, regulation by federal and state banking agencies and income taxation by the federal government and probably by the state, county and local governments. Your money is secured only by a highly touted but quite limited guarantee. If you put your money in a certificate of deposit or some other banking instrument, you subject yourself to penalties and withdrawal limitations. If you wish to access your money you have to relinquish its earning potential.

Mutual funds, stocks and bonds and other securities are regulated by the SEC. The registered reps who sell these investments are further subject to regulation by FINRA (formerly the NASD). These regulations determine what investments a registered rep can present to you and even the words that can be used when these offerings are discussed.

Gains from these investments are subject to a complex set of tax rules that keep attorneys and accountants in spending money. Turning an investment into money is not always an easy or pleasant task, especially when the investment is worth less than you paid for it. Taxation, regulation, limited access to your money: it's a mess.

State insurance departments regulate and control how whole life insurance policies are issued and how agents are licensed. The federal government and other regulators do not have any jurisdiction. This decentralized regulation allows for local oversight and better control. Therefore, the money you deposit into a traditional whole life insurance policy is not subject to the same limitations or cumbersome regulations as investments. Moreover, it is often better protected by state insurance funds than money in the bank or in an investment.

The growth within a traditional whole life insurance policy is not taxed. Dividends from participating policies are paid into the policy tax free and once paid into the policy become a permanent part of the policy. In addition, the money you put into a traditional whole life insurance policy, including any dividends that are paid in, continues to grow tax free as long as it remains in the policy.

Finally, you — and you alone — decide when and how you want to take money out of the policy and the terms upon which you may wish to redeposit that money. Once a policy is issued, *not even the insurance company that issues a traditional whole life insurance policy can tell you how to manage it* beyond the terms spelled out in the policy.

The Dazzling Dozen – No. 3

Reason number three why you and every money-smart person should choose to build your personal economy with participating whole life insurance at its core:

Your whole life insurance policy is protected from creditors and lawsuits.[2]

Every asset you own is at risk in a lawsuit, especially a lawsuit that involves creditors. Some assets may not be directly at risk, but, if you are unable to protect all of your assets, the one's you can protect end up having to work a lot harder to support your needs and wants.

One of the fundamental tenets of good planning is to make certain that your money structures can handle the planned and the unexpected events in your life. If you become disabled or are involved in an accident that you caused, you might find everything you own at risk.

Having a substantial amount of money in whole life insurance policies offers a level of protection that you will not find elsewhere. In addition to the protections that many

---

2   This document does not provide legal advice. Protections are not the same in every state and may not be available in some states. Consult an attorney about the laws in your state

states afford life insurance values, a qualified **Money for Life Guide**[3] is able to advise you about the benefits that various policy ownership arrangements can provide in this regard.

Having said that, it is imperative to involve competent legal and accounting advisors in your financial decision-making; not because they are expert in helping you choose insurance or investment products — they usually are not — but to assure yourself that you are taking maximum advantage of the legal and tax protections that are available.

It is important to note that the best practice guidelines for each professional specialty clearly delineate the roles of the advisor in that specialty; attorneys deal in law, accountants in taxation, registered reps in investments and insurance professionals in risk management.

---

3 http://www.EUREKONOMICS.com/find-an-advisor.html.

The Dazzling Dozen – No. 4

Reason number four why you and every money-smart person should choose to build your personal economy with participating whole life insurance at its core:

You can borrow against your whole life policy for any reason and you don't have to qualify in any way.

You own some real estate. You have a substantial amount of equity in the property. You want or need to borrow against that equity. Does the bank say "Sure, how much do you want?" Certainly not... The bank wants you to complete an application, pass a credit scoring test, pay a bunch of fees, submit to an appraisal and pay them a significant amount of interest — frequently up front.

If you own investments or savings and you want to borrow the money that's in them you'll have to jump through a similar set of hoops. If you aren't interested in doing that, you can liquidate those assets and convert them into money.

If you own participating whole life insurance — your *EUREKONOMICS™ bank* — you can borrow almost down to the last penny with a phone call or a stroke of your pen; no qualification required and no income to report; no hassle. In addition, you can choose your own repayment schedule and, since you are completely in charge, if you want to skip a payment or just pay interest for a while or pay nothing for a period of time, go right ahead. It's your *bank* and you're in charge.

Of course, if you never repay yourself you will eventually have to close your *bank* and lose all of the benefits you derive from having it.

Here's an example. A dear friend moved to Costa Rica to be with his dying grandmother and decided to stay there and start a real estate career. I didn't have any plans to visit but as I got deeper into the writing of *Money for Life*[4] I discovered that I needed a break. Since I missed my friend and it was a cold January in Denver my wife and I decided to visit Costa Rica. We borrowed the money we needed for the trip from our *bank* and off we went. It was a great vacation. We've paid this loan back and are thinking about doing it again in February 2011.

---

4   ©2008 Money for Life...How to thrive in good times and bad, Jeffrey Reeves, MA, Poor Richard Publishing Company, Denver, CO

The Dazzling Dozen – No. 5

Reason number five why you and every money-smart person should choose to build your personal economy with participating whole life insurance at its core:

When you borrow from your whole life policy, the money in your policy keeps growing as if you hadn't borrowed a cent…your money does double duty.

If you borrow equity from your home or you use investments as collateral for a loan, you pay interest and principle to a lender. The lender improves its earnings and its balance sheet. You may or may not see such an improvement.

Even if you prudently invest the money you borrow or spend it on appreciating assets you are faced with the costs of borrowing, with the costs of investing and with the significant risks that accompany both. When the cost of a loan goes up or the earnings on an investment go down as the real estate market did over the past several years and as the stock market did in 2002 and 2009 — or both happen at the same time — your "plan" sinks into the quicksand that is the underpinning of these strategies.

When you borrow from a participating whole life insurance policy — your EUREKONOMICS™ *bank* — the policy continues to grow in value and to pay dividends even with a loan outstanding. As you repay the loan — just as you would have to repay another lender — your cash value account restores itself to its original value.

If what you purchased with the money you borrowed from yourself loses all of its value, you still recover all of the money you borrowed from your *bank*. If your purchase proves a winner you recover all of your money and realize a gain. Whether you win or lose on the investment side — you win on the loan because *you are the bank* and your money works, doing double duty even when you borrow it. No other reservoir for money can *honestly* make that claim.

Here's an example. A client (we'll call her Mary) built up a $50,000.00 cash value in her participating whole life insurance policy — her EUREKONOMICS™ *bank*. A small house in her neighborhood, which had been occupied by a widow for over 60 years, became available when the widow died. Mary had been a kind neighbor and had befriended the older woman so the children, who wanted to settle the estate quickly, offered to sell the house to Mary at well below market value.

Mary didn't wish to borrow the money from a commercial bank so she negotiated to buy the house with a $25,000.00 down payment if the children of the widow would carry the balance until she could update it and sell it. They agreed. Mary borrowed the $25,000 from her whole life insurance policy. She used the other $25,000.00 in her policy to bring the house up to snuff. She sold it three months later and made a nifty $50,000.00 profit after repaying the $50,000.00 she had borrowed from her policy.

The Dazzling Dozen – No. 6

Reason number six why you and every money-smart person should choose to build your personal economy with participating whole life insurance at its core:

Using participating whole life insurance as your EUREKONOMICS™ program allows you to return the principal and interest you pay to purchase cars, household furnishings, vacations and other big ticket items or to fund education, business start-ups or any other costly expense to your EUREKONOMICS™ *bank*[5].

When you borrow money from a conventional lender you are *giving your money away*. The money you derived from the sweat, blood and tears of your work becomes the property of another in an unfair exchange. Here's what I mean.

Let's say you want to buy a new refrigerator. You go to the big box store and find just what you want for $3,000.00. Better yet, you can buy it today and pay no interest for a year. Such a deal. The year goes by; you pay the $3,000.00 and avoid the interest. The big box store makes a profit. You feel good with your decision. Everyone wins. Right?

---

5   This is a technical process unique to properly structured participating whole life insurance policies and require guidance from a qualified agent.

Wrong.

You gave your money away and in return got a depreciated asset that was immediately worth less than you paid for it. What really happens is this: the big box store is in cahoots with the finance company. They could sell the $3,000 item for $2,700, and still make a profit. Instead, they sell your I.O.U. to the finance company for $2,700, make their profits and a profit for the finance company too. You pay for all of it. You've helped make the store and its finance company richer and yourself poorer.

As an alternative, if you use available cash value in a participating whole life insurance policy, you can borrow the money from your policy, pay cash, and then repay your policy loan the same as you would the big box store finance company. Moreover, the big box store would likely give you a discount for paying cash. You'd pay the $2700 they need to make a profit. In the end, you would have the refrigerator *and the money too.* In fact, you'd have more money because you would also have been contributing premiums to your policy during the repayment period to enhance its value as you *bank.* Once you returned the money you spent on the refrigerator to your whole life policy, you could finance the 60" flat screen TV you are dreaming of.

Repeat this cycle for 20, 30 or 40 years in a row and you will *own* everything you need and anything you want without incurring a single debt-to-others.

The Dazzling Dozen – No. 7

Reason number seven why you and every money-smart person should choose to build your personal economy with participating whole life insurance at its core:

Your EUREKONOMICS™ program allows you to deposit all of the interest you would normally pay to credit card companies, banks and other credit grantors into your whole life insurance policy where it compounds for your benefit.

When you borrow money from a commercial lender to make a purchase and pay interest, you make two others richer; the seller of the product and the seller of the financing. When you use your *bank* to purchase the items you need and want you are able to reclaim not only the principle you would otherwise *give away* but also the interest that you would contribute to a lender's balance sheet and earnings statement.

This is not a trivial issue. The typical American family pays up to 35% of its gross earnings as interest on top of what they pay in true taxes; not just income taxes to federal, state and local governments but also Social Security and Medicare taxes plus taxes on gasoline, phone service, property, sales, etc. When you buy things with credit you frequently finance the taxes too — a double whammy.

When you borrow from your participating whole life insurance policy — your *bank* — and repay what you borrow (including the built-in taxes) you also recover the interest in your *bank* that would otherwise end up in the coffers of some lender and the bonus of the CEO who figured out how to get your money for his or her Behemoth. The interest you save over your lifetime with this simple strategy can, almost all by itself, make you wealthy.

Here's an example. If you buy ten autos, one every four years, and finance $26,000.00 each time through a local bank, you will spend almost $300,000.00 on cars. The bank that finances those autos will make almost double that amount off the money you pay them.

If you were to finance those same ten autos using your own EUREKONOMICS™ *bank*, you would put exactly the same amount of money into the hands of the auto company but — and this is the interesting thing about interest — you would recover every penny you spent, collect all of the interest you would otherwise have paid some commercial bank and would have almost $500,000.00 cash value in your participating whole life insurance policy.[6]

---

6   This example uses a policy for a healthy thirty-two year old woman. Speak with your agent about how this stategy would work for you.

The Dazzling Dozen – No. 8

Reason number eight why you and every money-smart person should choose to build your personal economy with participating whole life insurance at its core:

Your EUREKONOMICS™ program allows you to pre-pay the cost of future health and long-term care so the money you need as you age is in your whole life insurance policy when you need it most.

One of the greatest challenges we face is being able to care for ourselves or to be able to afford to pay for the care we need as we age. A three year stay in a nursing home (that's the average for one person) costs almost $200,000.00 today. Receiving the same care at home is just as expensive. Add to that the medical care costs that are not covered by long term care or Medicare insurance (Fidelity Funds estimate for a 65 year old couple in 2007 is $207,000.00). That's over $400,000.00 in unfunded medical and long term care costs for the typical retired couple, during their retirement.

This is a big problem for each of us and for society. If retired persons can't pay for their care then society will have to chip in. It is imperative to put money aside to pay for these costs. But, it is a daunting task in the conventional way of thinking.

It's not as scary if you use participating whole life insurance as your *bank*. The same participating whole life insurance policies that allow you to build your wealth by borrowing and repaying yourself for the things you buy throughout your lifetime can also be used to pay for unreimbursed medical expenses and long term care when you are older. Remember, everything you buy and pay for by borrowing from your EUREKONOMICS™ *bank* is going to be there for you when you are older. The more successful you are at building your *bank* in your early years, the more comfortable you'll be when you are older.

There is one other way to pay for post retirement medical and long term care costs; Health Savings Accounts. These vehicles allow you to put money aside for medical expenses during your working years. If there is money left in these accounts when you retire, you can use it to pay for unreimbursed medical expenses as well as long term care expenses or insurance premiums. You can also use these funds to pay for long term care insurance during your working years.

> *You can be young without money but you can't be old without it.* ~ Tennessee Williams

The Dazzling Dozen – No. 9

Reason number nine why you and every money-smart person should choose to build your personal economy with participating whole life insurance at its core:

Your whole life insurance policy can fund an inflation-protected income that you do not have to work for and you can't outlive.

You hear a lot of talk about "passive income" in the financial press and from investment advisors. Passive income is income that you don't have to work for. It is generally considered to derive from investments such as real estate, stocks, bonds and mutual funds. There's an unspoken problem that accompanies this thinking. This kind of passive income can be missing in action if you need it during a down market, when a real estate bubble bursts or if your situation demands cash and the only way to get it is by selling the asset you are relying on for passive income. In other words, it's risky and you can outlive it.

I recently had a call from an 81 year old gentleman seeking advice. He was nearly destitute. His medical expenses had eroded his assets beyond his expectations. All he had was his Social Security check and a small money market account to help him pay his bills. The assets he relied on for his passive income were gone. That gentleman was a successful financial advisor for most of his adult career. He had followed his own advice.

He found it wanting in wisdom.

The money you hold in a participating whole life insurance contract can be converted into income that you do not have to work for, that adjusts with inflation and that you cannot outlive. In addition, much of the income you derive when you take it from your policy can be free of income taxation.[7]

---

7 In fact, any asset that has market value can be converted this way. Many advisors, however, are not trained to accomplish this or work for Behemoths who advocate against this strategy and the cash value life insurance and annuity products that support it.

The Dazzling Dozen – No. 10

Reason number ten why you and every money-smart person should choose to build your personal economy with participating whole life insurance at its core:

You have ready access to the money in your EUREKONOMICS™ program when an unforeseen life event throws you off track (and that happens to everyone at some time or another.)

Conventional wisdom — *which is no wisdom at all* — tells you that you need six months income in the bank to cover emergencies. Bunk! That's a shibboleth — a false statement that has been repeated so many times that everyone assumes it is true. In 1492 the world was flat.

Ask any 50 something worker that has been caught in a downsizing if six months is enough. Three years later he or she could be a Wal-Mart greeter because there is no other option. How about the 27 year old that is partially paralyzed in a skiing accident and is looking forward to a two year rehab with lots of expense and no income? Consider the 38 year old widow with three children and only a small life insurance benefit, a mortgage beyond her ability to pay and a wonderfully inadequate six month reserve.

Take a look around and recognize that there are hundreds of situations that could require three, four or five years of ready cash. When you are younger and your responsibilities are fewer you might be able to get by a job loss or other minor events with a six month reserve. As you grow older, enter relationships, have children, incur mortgage debt… you know the rest.

This problem is made worse as you age and take on more responsibility. Conventional wisdom advises you to put your money in places where it is exposed to high levels of risk; where you either can't get to it or where it is costly to do so. It ignores your need for ready cash. The money in your participating whole life insurance policy. EUREKONOMICS™ is easy to get to. You can start accumulating this kind of ready money any time, but, the earlier in life that you begin, the more secure your future will be.

This foolishness about ready money endures because there are few advisors in the country that both understand and embrace the approach described in *Money for Life… How to thrive in good times and bad.* The Behemoths don't actively support this model because they don't have the financial products to implement it and because what they really want is to control as much of your money as they can.

I recently read an article by an advisor from one such firm that referred to clients as "wallets" — as in, "I want to control all of the money in their wallets."

The Dazzling Dozen – No. 11

Reason number eleven why you and every money-smart person should choose to build your personal economy with participating whole life insurance at its core:

Your EUREKONOMICS™ program lets you grow your wealth tax free every year…no sliding backward…no worries about stock market crashes or real estate market bubbles…just peace of mind about your money.

If your fortune was tied to the stock market in 2001, especially if you were heavily invested in the high tech stocks and mutual funds, you probably lost seventy-five percent of your money. I have developed clients over the past six or seven years who have still not recovered from their 2001–2002 losses.

> » A single woman in her late fifties who went from over $200,000.00 to less than $100,000.00 and is still not back to where she was.
> » A couple that went from $2,000,000.00 to under $800,000.00 and will never get back to their high point because they were retiring and had to figure out how to make the money that was left last a lifetime.

If you were in the real estate business in 2007-2010 and beyond and have properties that you planned to sell, you may be in for some financial surprises as the credit market contracts and your potential buyers find financing less available.

Ask a FINRA registered securities rep if there is any guarantee that your money will be there in seven — or seventeen or twenty-seventy or any-seven — years. There is none. No-one in the investment business is even allowed to use the word "guarantee." They'll quote lots of statistics about market performance over five, ten and twenty year spans and reassure you that everything will be OK. They will not promise anything.

The money in your participating whole life insurance policy — EUREKONOMICS™ — is guaranteed by the insurance company and backed by fifty state insurance guarantee funds. Not only is it guaranteed to be there when you need it, it is guaranteed to increase in value every year and the IRS says that the increase is tax free.

Don't draw the implication from this brief commentary that investing is wrong or advisors are leading you astray. Advocating for prudence does not invalidate investing. The aim is to find a secure place for money that allows you to launch an investment program and manage the risk too.

The Dazzling Dozen – No. 12

Reason number twelve why you and every money-smart person should choose to build your personal economy with participating whole life insurance at its core:

EUREKONOMICS™ serves you without compromise while you are alive and allows you to pay forward — tax free and to anyone you choose — your legacy of both your wealth and your wisdom.

During your lifetime your whole life insurance policy finances your purchases, earns a steady, tax free, and guaranteed return, pays dividends tax free, supports you when you experience the unexpected, secures your health care for later in life, helps you achieve financial goals, protects your money from lawsuits and bill collectors, let's you do all of that and more on your own terms without the intrusion of employers, Behemoths or the government.

"But wait!" as the TV pitchman says, "There's more!"

When you die — and we all die — your participating whole life insurance policies close their doors and distribute your money: **Tax free, to whomever you choose.**

If you have had the good sense and the good heart to teach others about *EUREKONOMICS™*, then your legacy is much more than just money. You will have created a new generation of wisdom-holders who will propagate your contribution to the world and to generation upon generation in your name.

This is the ultimate goal of EUREKONOMICS™. Sure the authors want to earn money from book sales and speaking engagements and to attract new clients. We want to build our *bank* too.

More importantly, however, we want to pass on the wisdom of generations from millennia gone by; to know that those who adopt the practices from *EUREKONOMICS*™ will "breathe easier" and experience peace of mind about money.

You can help.

Tell a few of your friends and relatives about:
>> the book, *Money for Life…How to thrive in good times and bad*
>> the blog — www.TheMoneyForLifeBlog.com
>> the web site — www.EUREKONOMICS.com.

The Dazzling Dozen – Epilogue

Sometimes it may sound like I am coming across as the enemy of financial professionals and the investment community. That is not the case. I personally rely on a Certified Financial Planning Professional to manage the money that I borrow from my whole life insurance policies and leverage into investments.

This approach to investing is normally quite successful and profitable. Those who adopt it are consistently able to repay their whole life insurance policy loans and keep their investment portfolio growing.

The value of using participating whole life insurance as your fundamental money management tool and resource is that it is safe, reliable, versatile and flexible. It allows you to pursue any investment you desire knowing that you will return the money you are taking from your whole life insurance policy. Even if the investment is a complete failure, your *policy* will be restored.

PEACE OF MIND.

May your life be filled with
Health, Abundance, Love and Light.

About Jeffrey Reeves MA...

Jeffrey Reeves is the creator of EUREKONOMICS™. Jeffrey is a licensed life insurance agent and a recovering registered securities rep. He has been guiding clients for nearly forty years as they chart their paths to financial security. During this time, the words of Benjamin Franklin and dozens of other American authors and financial writers, individuals and small business owners have all contributed ideas, strategies and tactics to the arsenal of tools that emerge throughout Jeffrey's books, blogs, articles, and web sites.

These contributions offer the reader an extraordinary wealth of insight, knowledge and just plain old common sense about money. Although creativity allowed these ideas to come together as a coherent message, they remain the common property of all Americans.

EUREKONOMICS™ Books

EUREKONOMICS™ —a term coined by Jeffrey Reeves, combines the power of two ancient Greek words into a unique 21st century term.

Eureka means "I found it!" Oikonomia, economy in English, means "household management."

Amazingly—and unfortunately—the original meaning of economy has been lost. A volcanic eruption of misinformation and disinformation over the past half century buried the idea that Americans are responsible for their own personal economies.

Order your copy of *Money for Life...How to thrive in good times and bad* - a complete education in the Money for Life principles and practices. The book...

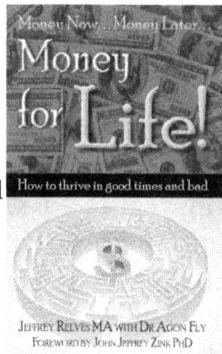

- Introduces the villians that survive and thrive by consuming your money for their own benefit.
- Discusses the myths, misrepresentations, and misconceptions of the current failed financial model.
- Defines and describes "personal economy" and shows why every American needs one.
- Studies the financial models that ruled America's economy from the founding of the country and evolved into the failed model that America adopted in the late 20th century.
- Looks at the underpinnings of the Debt Paradigm and insight into how to escape it.
- Discusses how you can free yourself from the dungeon of the Debt Paradigm and introduces cash value life insurance as the preferred "*bank*ing" vehicle in the Money for Life financial model.
- Describes the Four Pillars that support EVERY successful personal economy. Contains extensive and detailed examples drawn from clients and experience of over 30 years.
- Demonstrates how you can deconstruct and reconstruct your personal economy and free up money. Contains several examples, from real life situations, of individuals and families moving from dependence to independence.

The Way to Wealth by Benjamin Franklin
with Commentary by Dr Agon Fly

In 1758, Benjamin Franklin published the 25th and final issue of Poor Richard's Almanac. As a preface to this final edition, he wrote *The Way to Wealth* and introduced Father Abraham as the main character in the tale. Father Abraham embodied the financial wisdom that "Poor" Richard Saunders —one of Benjamin Franklin's many pen names —incorporated in the 25 years during which the almanac was a staple on mantels above fireplaces, in personal libraries and on the tables of colonial America.

In 2008, on the 250th anniversary year of that event, Dr Agon Fly is adding a unique and timely perspective to this classic book about money and life. The wisdom that Dr. Benjamin Franklin captured in *The Way to Wealth* is timeless. However, the vernacular of 1758 sometimes obscures the meaning for today's economy and for the personal economies of 21st Century Americans. Dr Agon Fly's commentary adds clarity to the language and insights found in The Way to Wealth's tested and true principles and practices. A Commentary on Benjamin Franklin's classic *The Way to Wealth*.

R. Nelson Nash praises this work in his Foreword to The *Way to Wealth,* where he states that the "commentary ranks right alongside George Clason's *The Richest Man in Babylon* as the complete answer to the problems created by the arrogance of the financial community during our times…"

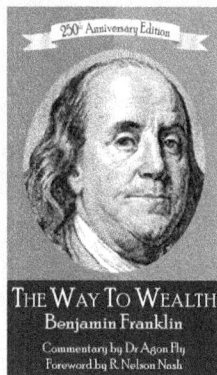

Order both at www.EUREKONOMICS.com

Every American that wonders about their financial future should own a copy of...

The Five Great Gifts of Whole Life Insurance.

"Why?" you ask.

During the past forty years, the Behemoths of Wall Street and Washington tried to bury the knowledge, understanding, and wisdom of whole life insurance under an onslaught of disinformation and misinformation from their cohorts on Madison Avenue.

Their aim?

To gain control of money that rightly belongs to Americans, to their families, and to small businesses.

The Behemoths succeeded in taking millions of Americans down a path that leads to financial servitude. However, they failed to damage the companies and insurance professionals that know what Americans really want, understand how whole life insurance really works...really, and why it belongs at the foundation or every personal economy.

The power, flexibility, and versatility of participating whole life insurance has served and saved the personal economies American families for over one hundred-fifty years.

Whether you are a single person, member of a family, matriarch, patriarch, owner of a business, executive at a large company, or an insurance and financial advisor—providing those you care about with their personal copy of *The Five Great Gifts of Whole Life Insurance* is a service they will remember—and appreciate—for a long time.

Contact us at **admin@EUREKONOMICS.com**.

Or call 888-300-9661 for more information.

We will show you how you can economically create a *customized* version of the unique book to pay forward its wealth of wisdom.